WORLD MYTHS
AND LEGENDS

Native American

Joanne Suter

Fearon/Janus
Belmont, CA

Simon & Schuster Supplementary Education Group

World Myths and Legends

Greek and Roman
Ancient Middle Eastern
Norse
African
Far Eastern
Celtic
Native American
Regional American

Series Editor: Joseph T. Curran
Cover Designer: Dianne Platner
Text Designer: Teresa A. Holden
Interior Illustrations: James Balkovek
Cover Photo: Lowie Museum of Anthropology,
  The University of California at Berkeley

Library of Congress Catalog Card Number: 91-72590

ISBN 0-8224-4640-5

Printed in the United States of America

1. 9 8 7 6 5 4 3 2

CONTENTS

An Introduction to Native American Myths and Legends

Most historians believe the first people came to the Americas about 25,000 years ago. Hunters probably crossed a land bridge that stretched across the Bering Strait from Siberia to Alaska. They gradually moved south across North America and Central America until they reached the very tip of South America.

The earliest Americans had no written language. Storytelling kept their history, religion, and traditions alive. It produced a wealth of myths and legends.

The myths are the oldest stories. They have roots in ancient tribal religious beliefs. The myths describe the creation of the world and of the animals and people who live in it. They speak of life and death and of good and evil.

The legends were added later. They include stories of tricksters and heroes. These, too, reflect the values of the people who told them.

The myths and legends have many different geographical settings. These include frozen coastlands, steamy jungles, open plains, dense woodlands, and rugged mountain ranges.

Stories from different regions have their own distinct flavors. But there are common threads in Native American mythology. Many creation myths say the world was made of mud that was brought up from beneath vast waters. And trickster tales are told throughout the Americas. They describe a time when animals could talk and could make the world respond to their wishes.

The word *spirit* appears again and again in these stories. It refers to the power that dwells in all of nature. Mountains, rivers, and stars weren't thought of simply as objects. They were full of life. To view the world in this way is to have great respect for it.

Some of these stories are filled with sorrow, others with joy. Some show the harsh side of life, while others celebrate beauty and peace. The stories were born in the hearts, minds, and souls of the earliest Americans. They help us know what it means to be of this land.

Tribes of the Americas

Myths and legends of the following groups of people appear in this book.

Apinaye. The Apinaye lived in the Brazilian highlands and spoke a language known as *Ge*. They were hunters and gatherers. They also raised yams, corn, and other crops in semi-permanent villages.

Aztec. The Aztecs built the last great native civilization in Mexico before the country was colonized by Spain. The Aztecs built pyramid-style temples. They were skilled potters, weavers, and jewelers. They developed a form of picture-writing and a calendar stone to record the passage of time.

When Montezuma II held the Aztec throne, he demanded tributes from all the people in his realm. These tributes included gold, silver, and humans who were sacrificed to the gods.

At first, the Aztecs welcomed the Spaniards, thinking them divine. They discovered their mistake too late and were defeated in 1521.

Brule Sioux. The Brules were one of the seven western Sioux tribes of the North American plains. The Sioux made up a huge nation and were at first friendly to the white newcomers. Later they fought fiercely to defend their hunting grounds.

The Brules were a very traditional people. Despite outside influences, they kept their own customs and rituals.

Cherokee. The Cherokee lived in the mountains of western North Carolina, eastern Tennessee, northeastern Alabama, and northern Georgia. The Cherokee, more than any other southern tribe, adapted to the lifestyles of the white settlers. They learned to farm in the manner of their white neighbors. They modeled their government after the United States government.

Before long, however, the United States government decided to take over the rich and fertile Cherokee lands. In 1838, some 13,000 Cherokees were forced to move west. A third of them died in a march remembered as the Trail of Tears.

Choctaw. The Choctaws lived in Mississippi and western Alabama. They were peace-loving farmers and traders. Their language became the trading language used across the South. It was spoken between different native tribes and between natives and whites.

Creek. The Creeks lived in what is today Georgia and Alabama. The Creek nation was made up of many small tribes. The tribes banded together to protect themselves and their lands against white settlers and white armies. The Creeks maintained their traditions longer than any other southern tribe.

Eskimo. The Eskimos lived in the harsh climates of the far north, around the Arctic coasts of Alaska, Canada, and Greenland. They fished, and they hunted seals, whales, walrus, and caribou. During the summer months, Eskimos lived in skin tents. In winter, they built more permanent dwellings out of stone, wood and turf. Some Eskimos also built domed snowhouses called *igloos*.

Haida. The Haida people lived on Queen Charlotte Island off the coast of British Columbia. They hunted whales and sea otters. The Haida were artists and carvers. They were known for the totems, canoes, and elaborately decorated wooden homes they built.

Huron. The Hurons lived along the St. Lawrence River. They were mainly farmers, but they also fished. Huron men cleared fields that the women then planted and harvested. Huron leaders were chosen by women.

Karok. The Karok lived along the Klamath River in northern California and southern Oregon. They were seed gatherers and salmon fishers. Because there were no redwood trees in their area, they could not build their own canoes. So they bought canoes from their neighbors to the south, the Yurok.

Kiowa. The Kiowa were buffalo-hunters of the southwestern plains. They raided cattle ranches in Texas and kept records of their deeds on painted buffalo skins. The Kiowa were famous for their colorful tribal dances.

Maidu. The Maidu were a northern California tribe. The earliest Maidu were seed gatherers. They now live north of San Francisco Bay and are known for the elaborate baskets they weave.

Modoc. The Modoc lived along the lower Klamath Lake in southwestern Oregon. They fought long and hard when the government tried to force them onto reservations. When they were at last forced to surrender, part of the tribe was moved to Indian territory in Oklahoma. Others were placed on the Klamath Reservation.

Multnomah. The Multnomah tribe lived in what is now western Oregon, near Portland. They were a peaceful people who fished the area's rivers and lakes. Today the few remaining Multnomah people have almost entirely blended with the white cultures surrounding them.

Ojibwa. The Ojibwa lived in eastern Canada around Lake Superior. They traded with the French, swapping beaver and other pelts for firearms. Today the Ojibwa live on a number of reservations, most of which are in Minnesota.

Seminole. The Seminoles were made up of various groups that fled to Florida in the late 1700s. Many of them left the Creek federation and were escaping war and other troubles with the whites. Later, other native Americans as well as slaves from southern plantations found safety with the Seminoles.

Tupari. The Tupari lived along the Rio Branco in Brazil. They believed in magic and, until 1948, had virtually no contact with outside civilizations.

Wasco. The Wasco were a group of fishing people who lived along the banks of the Columbia River in Oregon. They caught salmon, sturgeon, and eels. They were famous for their beautiful twined baskets. Today the Wasco live on the Warm Springs Reservation in Oregon.

Earth Starter

Myths often ask more questions than they answer. In this Maidu story, humans are given the secret of eternal youth. The first man goes into a lake and comes out young again. What happened to that secret of rebirth? Were people too frightened to follow the first man into the lake? Did they forget to do as the creator told them?

The World

In the beginning it was dark, and there was water everywhere. Then a raft appeared from the north. Turtle and Pehe-ipe were aboard the raft.

The two sat quietly until a rope of feathers came down from the sky. Earth Starter climbed down that rope. He tied its end to the raft and climbed aboard to join Turtle and Pehe-ipe.

Earth Starter's body was shining, but his face was covered. Turtle and Pehe-ipe could not see what he looked like. They knew he was a god, however.

"Where do you come from?" Turtle asked.

"I come from above," said Earth Starter.

"We have floated on the water for such a long time," Turtle said. "Could you make us some dry land?"

"I understand what you seek," said Earth Starter. "But where am I to get the earth to make it?"

Turtle had an idea. "Tie a rope around my leg," he said. "I'll dive under the water and search for some earth. When I jerk the rope, pull me up quickly. I'll carry all the earth I can hold."

So Earth Starter took the end of the rope of feathers and untied it from the raft. He looped it around Turtle's leg. Then Turtle jumped into the water.

Immediately Pehe-ipe began to shout and scream, for he was afraid.

Turtle was gone for six years. At last Earth Starter felt a hard jerk on the rope, and he pulled Turtle back onto the raft. Turtle was covered with green slime.

"Where is the earth?" Earth Starter asked in alarm.

Turtle had just a little bit of earth stuck under his nails. The rest had all washed away. Earth Starter took a knife and scraped the earth from beneath Turtle's nails. He rolled it into a pebble-sized ball.

Turtle helping Earth Starter

Then he placed that tiny ball of earth on the deck of the raft.

Earth Starter watched the ball. At first, it didn't seem to change. But then it began growing. It grew and grew until it was as big as the world. The raft soon got stuck on dry land.

Earth Starter, Turtle, and Pehe-ipe got off the raft.

"It is quite dark!" said Turtle. "Can't you make some light?"

"I'll tell my sister to come up," Earth Starter said. "Look there, in the east."

A light began to glow. The Sun came up, and the first day dawned. Pehe-ipe shouted.

"Look, the Sun is moving," said Turtle.

"She will pass above us and go down over there," said Earth Starter. He pointed to the western part of the sky.

When the Sun went down, it grew dark again. Pehe-ipe began to wail and cry. So Earth Starter called the stars out.

Earth Starter's sister, the Sun, came back the next day. It became very hot, and Pehe-ipe started to cry. So Earth Starter made a great oak tree. The three of them sat in its shade for two days. Then they went off to explore the world.

1. *On what did Earth Starter climb down to the raft?*

2. *Why did Turtle dive into the water?*

3. *Who was Earth Starter's sister?*

Animals and People

While Earth Starter, Turtle, and Peheipe were exploring, Coyote and his dog, who was named Rattlesnake, came up from the ground to join them. Coyote was the only one who was allowed to see Earth Starter's actual face.

Earth Starter began making creatures for the world. He took mud and made the first deer. Then he made the other animals. Turtle wanted a hand in the work. More than once he said, "That doesn't look right. Make it this way."

Pretty soon Earth Starter told Coyote something. "I think I am going to some make people," he said.

He mixed some red earth with water. He formed a man and a woman. He laid the man beside him to the right. He laid the woman beside him to the left. Then Earth Starter lay flat on his back with his arms outstretched. He lay that way all day and all night.

Early the next morning, the woman began to tickle Earth Starter. But Earth Starter lay very still and did not laugh.

The first man and woman came to life. Earth Starter called the first man Ku'ksu. Then he named the first woman Morning-star Woman.

"*I* want to make some people!" Coyote said. "It doesn't look all that hard." So Coyote took some red earth and mixed it with water just as Earth Starter had done. Then he laid the forms beside him. But when the woman tickled Coyote's side, Coyote couldn't help but laugh. And since he couldn't stay quiet, the people did not come to life.

"What is wrong with my people?" he complained to Earth Starter.

"Did you laugh when the woman tickled you?" Earth Starter asked him.

"No," said Coyote. This was the first lie told in the world.

As time passed, many people were created. Earth Starter liked his people, and he wanted things to be good for them. He decided to show them a trick.

Earth Starter went to see Ku'ksu. "Tomorrow morning," he said, "go to the lake near here. Take all the people with you."

So the people traveled to the lake, but by the time they got there Ku'ksu was an old man. He was so frail he could hardly stand. Ku'ksu fell into the lake and sank from sight.

Then the ground began to shake, and there was a roaring like thunder.

Ku'ksu came back up from under the water. He was a young man again.

Earth Starter said to the people, "Always do as I say, and everything will be good. When you grow old, you must come quickly to this lake. You must go down under the water just as Ku'ksu did. Then you will come up young again."

Saying these words, Earth Starter went up into the sky. And that is where he stayed.

4. *What did Earth Starter use to form the first man and woman?*

5. *Why didn't Coyote's people come to life?*

6. *How had Ku'ksu changed when he came up out of the water?*

The Divine Woman

Here's another creation myth that takes place in a watery world. In this one, too, earth is taken from beneath the water to make dry land.

In the beginning there was water everywhere. Creatures swam in the water, but there was no dry land for them to crawl up on and rest.

Then a woman fell from a torn place in the sky. She was a divine woman, and was therefore full of power. Two loons that were flying by at the time caught her as she fell.

"Help us!" they cried to all the other creatures. "You must help us save the Divine Woman."

A snapping turtle came to help. The loons set the woman down on the turtle's back. Other water creatures swam in circles around the turtle.

"What we need," said Turtle, "is dry land for the woman to live on. Dive down into the water and bring up some earth."

So down went the beaver, the muskrat, the water snake, and some other swimming creatures. They were under the water a long

8

Turtle holds up the earth

time, and some of them died. When they
finally came up, Turtle looked inside their
mouths. But he could find no earth. Now the
Divine Woman was getting very heavy on
Turtle's back. He really needed some dry
ground to put her on.

At last a fat green toad came to the
surface. He had stayed under the water for
a long time, and now he was nearly dead.
But when Turtle looked inside Toad's
mouth, he found a little bit of earth.

The Divine Woman took this bit of earth
and smeared it on Turtle's shell. It grew and
grew until it became the world. To this day,
Turtle holds up the earth.

1. *Where did the Divine Woman fall from?*

2. *Where did the loons put the Divine Woman?*

3. *What animal finally brought up some earth to start the new world?*

The Sky Spirits

The Modocs say it is wrong to kill a grizzly bear. This creation myth tells of a time when grizzly bears walked on two legs and talked, just as people do.

A New Home

The Chief of the Sky Spirits lived with his family in the Above World.

"Brrr! It's cold here," his wife complained. The chief agreed with her. There was so much snow and ice that they were never able to get warm.

"Let me see what can be done," the Chief of the Sky Spirits said. He cut a hole in the sky and pushed all the snow and ice through it. It piled up into a great mountain. Today it is called Mount Shasta.

The chief looked down at the mountain he had created. Then he took his walking stick and stepped onto its peak. He began to walk down the mountain.

He poked his finger here and there. In every place he touched, a tree grew. The chief's footsteps melted the snow, and water ran in streams and rivers.

The chief broke off parts of his walking stick and threw them into the rivers. They turned into fish and swam away happily. He broke off bigger pieces of the stick, and they turned into beavers. Leaves fell from the trees, and when the chief breathed upon them they flew off as birds. Then the chief took the end of his stick and made all the world's animals.

The largest animals were the grizzly bears. They were covered with hair and had sharp claws. They walked around on two feet and talked, just like people. The grizzlies were fierce-looking, and the chief sent them to live in a forest at the foot of the mountain.

The chief was happy with all he had created. He fetched his family from the Above World and brought them down to live on earth. They made their home inside the mountain of snow and ice. The Chief of the Sky Spirits built a big fire in the center of their mountain lodge. Then he cut a hole in the top of the mountain in order to let out all the smoke.

"Put a fresh log on the fire," his wife would call to him. When the chief did this, the earth would shake and sparks would shoot out the top of the mountain.

The chief and his family were warm and happy in the mountain. But then one day the Wind Spirit blew up a great storm. Gusts of wind came down through the hole and threatened to put out the fire.

"Climb up to the hole and call to the Wind Spirit," the chief told his little daughter. "Tell him he's putting out our fire. Ask him to blow more gently."

The daughter started to climb up to the smoke hole. Her father called after her, "Don't stick your head out the hole. If you do, the wind may catch you, and it might blow you away."

The girl stayed well inside the mountain when she called to the Wind Spirit. After she had made her request, she started to climb back down. But she was young and curious and had never seen the earth outside her mountain home.

"Oh, how I'd love to see the land below us," she said. "I wonder what the forests and rivers are like." She quickly climbed back up to the hole. Then she peeked over the rim and looked to the west. In a second, the Wind Spirit caught her long red hair and blew her right out of the mountain. A strong gust carried her to the edge of the forest. There she lay, cold, frightened, and alone.

1. *Why did the chief and his family move down to earth?*

2. *How did the chief make trees grow?*

3. *How were the grizzly bears in this story different from real ones today?*

The Grizzlies

It wasn't long before a huge grizzly bear came across the girl. Fierce-looking as he was, the bear didn't harm her. Instead he picked her up and carried her home with him. His wife raised her, and the little red-haired girl became a sister to the grizzly cubs. She ate with them and wrestled with them. They were always careful not to hurt their weaker sister.

When the girl grew up, she married the oldest grizzly son. In time, they had babies. The children did not look like their father, for they had much less hair. But they didn't look exactly like their spirit mother, either.

Meanwhile, the grizzly bear mother had grown old. She knew that her time to die had come. And she felt badly about having kept the Chief of the Sky Spirits' daughter. "I must ask for forgiveness," she told her husband. So she sent one of her sons to the

Grizzly bear

top of Mount Shasta. He told the chief where to find his long-lost daughter.

The chief came hurrying to the forest. How surprised he was to see the grown-up woman his daughter had become. And how furious he was to see her children. They were a whole new race that he had not created. The Chief of the Sky Spirits turned on the grizzlies and shouted in anger, "Get down on your knees! You have stolen my child. From this moment on, you will walk on four feet and never again talk!"

Then the chief put his daughter over his shoulder and carried her back to the mountain. He never went back to the forest. Some say the chief put out the fire in the mountain and took all of his family back up to the sky.

The chief's grandchildren, who were born to his daughter and the grizzly, wandered over the earth. They were the first people, the ancestors of all the tribes. And that is why the people of Mount Shasta would never kill a grizzly bear.

4. *Who did the spirit girl marry when she grew up?*

5. *Why was the chief angry about the new race of beings?*

6. *How did the chief punish the grizzlies?*

Raven the Creator

The raven appears frequently in Native American mythology. In this story from Alaska, Raven is the creator.

In the beginning there were no people on earth. There was only a large black bird called Raven. Raven had created himself. At first the earth was bare and empty. But as Raven moved across the land, he left behind him a trail of trees, streams, and mountains. Everywhere Raven went, the earth became more beautiful.

One time Raven left behind him a giant pea pod vine. A single pod grew on this vine. For a long time, the pod hung there in stillness and silence.

Then it began to move. It trembled and shook. Something inside was struggling very hard to break free.

At last that something pushed through the bottom of the pod. It crawled out and stood up on two feet. It was the first man, full-grown and completely formed. The man looked around him and saw the broken pod hanging from the vine.

The first man walked a little ways away from the pod. *Squish, squish.* The man's feet sank into the ground, for it was very soft and wet. It moved when he stepped on it. The man didn't like this. He felt very unsafe.

The man stood still, afraid to walk any further. A pool of water formed around his feet. He bent down and scooped some of the water into his hand. He brought it to his lips and drank. It made him feel good.

Then the man saw a dark flapping thing coming toward him through the air. *Caw! Caw!* it called out.

When the thing reached him, it landed. It stood before him and looked him over from head to toe. It had a long sharp beak and black feathers. It was Raven.

"Who are you?" Raven asked the man. "Where did you come from?"

"I seem to have come from that pod," the man said as he pointed to the vine.

"I made that vine!" said Raven. "But I never thought such a thing as you would grow on it!"

The man took a step toward Raven. *Squish, squish.*

"Oh, I don't like this ground," the man said in disgust.

The first man and Raven

"Follow me up to higher ground," Raven told the man. "You will find it much firmer."

So the man followed Raven. They walked until the ground beneath their feet was firm.

"I don't feel well," the man said to Raven.

"Have you had anything to eat?" Raven asked him.

The man told him about the wet stuff he had tasted.

"That was water," Raven said. "You need something more. Wait here." Then Raven flew away.

The man waited a long time. He had nothing to do but wait. He had nowhere to go in this brand new world.

At last Raven returned. He dropped four berries in front of the man.

"I made these for you," Raven said to the man. "From now on they will grow all over the earth for you to eat."

The man ate the berries. "I feel better now," he said.

Then Raven led the man to a creek. There he took two pieces of clay and molded them into tiny animals. The animals had short legs and long horns. They were musk-oxen. Raven set them on the ground to dry.

When the clay figures were dry, Raven waved his wings over them. The musk-oxen sprang to life and grew in size. Then they turned and ran away.

The man was delighted with this new form of life. So Raven made more clay figures. He made all kinds of birds, fish, and animals. Then he showed the man how to make a bow and arrow. And he taught him how to hunt animals for food.

The man learned quickly. "I am much more clever than the animals!" he shouted. This worried Raven. Perhaps the man would try to kill and eat all the other creatures. Raven decided he had better create something Man would fear.

So Raven scooped up a big lump of clay. He shaped the clay into a bear. Raven brought the bear to life and then stood back, for it was huge and fierce.

The bear roared off out of sight. The man was glad to see it go.

Then Raven noticed that the man looked a little sad. "What is wrong?" he asked.

"None of these creatures look anything like me. None of them can talk to me."

"You are lonely," said Raven. "I will make somebody for you."

Then Raven made another form. It was very much like the man, but different. Raven put some long grass on its head.

When the figure had dried, he waved his wings over it, and it came to life. It was the first woman.

The woman grew to full size and then walked over and stood beside the man.

"She is very nice," the man said. He sounded much happier.

"She is the first woman," Raven told him.

Soon the man and the woman had a child. Raven took the baby to the stream and rubbed him all over with clay. This made him strong and healthy. He quickly grew into a full-sized man.

Meanwhile, more pods were growing on the vine. The pods held other men and women. Soon there were many people, and they wandered throughout the land. They learned to take care of themselves. They became skillful hunters. They built villages.

"Don't kill too many animals," Raven warned them again and again. In those earliest days, people listened to Raven's warning. And the world was a fine and wonderful place to be.

1. *What did Raven give the man to eat?*

2. *What did Raven use to make the animals?*

3. *Why did Raven create the bear?*

From Beneath the Earth

The Tupari lived along a river in Brazil called the Rio Branco. Like most native peoples of South America, the Tupari believed in what we would call magic. Here is their description of the first humans.

The Magicians

In the beginning there were no people on earth. There was only a big block of rock. It was shiny and beautiful. One day the block split. Out of it poured streams of blood and one man. This man was Valedjad.

Again the rock split. This time a second man came forth. His name was Vab. Valedjad and Vab were not mortal men. They were magicians.

The two magicians wanted wives. So they made two stone axes, and cut down two trees. Then they killed an *agouti*, a rat-like animal about the size of a rabbit. They took out the creature's two front teeth. From the teeth each magician carved a woman. Once Valedjad and Vab had wives, children could be born. Soon there were many other magicians on the earth.

Now Valedjad was a wicked magician. He often became very angry, and when he did so, it rained. Valedjad was angry so much of the time that one day the whole earth flooded. Many of the magicians were drowned. Those who escaped the flood knew that Valedjad had to be stopped.

A magician named Arkoanyo came up with a plan. He hid in a tree, and when Valedjad passed by, he poured liquid beeswax down on him. The wax sealed Valedjad's eyes and nose. It stuck his fingers together tightly.

Then a large bird seized Valedjad and carried him far away to the north. To this day Valedjad lives alone in a stone hut. He still gets angry, and when he does, heavy rains fall on the earth.

1. *What did the two magicians use to create their wives?*

2. *Which of the magicians was wicked?*

3. *What was Arkoanyo's plan?*

The First Tupari

In time, most of the magicians decided to go up to heaven to live. A few chose to stay on the ground. Those who left climbed up a vine that hung from the sky.

In those days, there were no mortals on the earth's surface. The first Tupari lived under the ground where the sun never shone. They had nothing to eat but some shriveled palm fruits. Therefore, they were always hungry.

One night some of the Tupari discovered a hole in the earth. They climbed up out of the hole not far from the tent of two magicians. The Tupari found peanuts and maize growing in the magicians' fields. Since they were so very hungry, they ate as much as they could. Then, with full bellies they went back down the hole.

Every night after that, the Tupari came up through the hole. They ate their fill and then disappeared beneath the earth again. At first the magicians thought the agoutis were stealing their crops. But then they saw the Tupari's tracks. The magicians followed the footprints until they came to the hole. They started digging and made the opening wider and wider. Suddenly a crowd of people began to stream out.

"Oh, no!" the magicians cried. "These creatures look horrible!" The people from beneath the earth had long sharp tusks like those of wild boars. They had webs between their fingers and toes. The magicians cornered the Tupari and snapped off their tusks. Then they cut the webs from their hands and feet.

All those who came up from under the earth couldn't live comfortably in only one place. So they wandered off in different directions. They formed tribes and gave themselves new names. Some stayed near the hole with the magicians who had decided to remain on the earth. These people kept the name Tupari.

4. *What did the Tupari eat when they came up out of the hole?*

5. *What animals did the magicians think were stealing their crops?*

6. *What was unusual about the people from beneath the earth?*

The Hungry Woman

The Aztecs established a great civilization in Mexico before the coming of the Spaniards. The two most important spirits in Aztec mythology were Quetzalcoatl and Tezcatlipoca. When the Spaniard Cortés came to Mexico in 1519, the Aztecs thought he was Quetzalcoatl. They welcomed him. They realized too late that he wasn't a god at all, but a conqueror.

Quetzalcoatl and Tezcatlipoca were male figures who played important roles in the Aztec creation story. But the Aztecs describe the world itself as being made from the body of a woman.

There was once a woman who continually cried for food. She was not an earthly woman, for as yet there was no earth. She dwelt in the place where the spirits lived.

"Food! Food!" she demanded. The words came out of mouths in her elbows and wrists. They came out of mouths in her knees and ankles.

"She can't eat here!" said the spirits. "She'll have to live somewhere else."

But above there was only empty air. And to the right and the left it was the same. However, when the spirits looked down, they saw what looked like water.

"If we put her below," the spirits said, "there will be plenty to eat and she'll be able to satisfy her hunger."

So Quetzalcoatl and Tezcatlipoca grabbed the hungry woman and dragged her down to the water.

When they tossed her in, her many mouths spluttered and gasped. But she was able to float.

Then Quetzalcoatl and Tezcatlipoca changed themselves into snakes. They wrapped themselves around the woman and squeezed. Before long she snapped in half.

"It looks like we squeezed too hard," they said. "What do we do with her now?" Not knowing what else to do, they carried the bottom half of the woman back to the spirit place and called a council.

"Don't worry," said the other spirits. "We can make good use of this." The spirits used the bottom half of the woman to make the vast beautiful sky.

Then the spirits flew down to where the top half of the woman was still floating. They began to make grass and flowers from her skin. They made forests from her hair and springs and pools from her eyes. From her shoulders they made mountains, and from her nose, valleys.

But just as before, the woman's mouths were everywhere. They were still crying for food, and still biting. And they still are. When it rains, she drinks. When flowers shrivel, when trees fall, or when someone dies, she eats. When people are killed in battle, she drinks their blood. Her mouths are always opening and snapping shut, and she never gets enough to eat. Sometimes at night her howling for food sounds just like the wind.

1. *Who dragged the hungry woman down to the water?*

2. *What did the spirits change themselves into when they got to the water?*

3. *What did the spirits make with the top and bottom halves of the woman's body?*

Why the Possum's Tail Is Bare

The animals that appear in early myths were superior to today's animals. They were very large and extremely clever. The Cherokee say that humans drove away those first animals by hunting and mistreating them. When the animals could stand it no longer, they took the rainbow path to the Sky Land. Smaller and weaker animals came after them.

In the old days, all the animals got along pretty well together. But sometimes there were quarrels. And sometimes the animals played tricks on each other. The rabbit, especially, liked to stir up trouble.

Now in those distant times, the possum had a long bushy tail. He was very proud of its thick black fur. Possum liked to spend his time combing and brushing his tail, and singing its praises for all to hear.

"See how I can raise it so high!" Possum sang. "See how I can wrap it around myself like a coat!"

Soon the animals grew tired of Possum's ravings about his tail.

Proud Possum

"I've had it!" said Rabbit one day. "I'm going to shut Possum up once and for all!" Actually, Rabbit was more than a little jealous of Possum's bushy tail. You see, Rabbit himself had once had a long furry tail. But during a fight, Bear had pulled it out. Since then, Rabbit had only a little puff of fur where his tail had been.

An important council meeting and feast was soon to be held. As usual, it was up to Rabbit to deliver invitations, for he was the animals' messenger. The coming feast gave Rabbit an idea.

He hurried to Possum's lodge to deliver the invitation. As usual, Possum was sitting by his door grooming his tail.

"Greetings!" Rabbit said to him. "I bring news of the great council meeting. Do you plan to attend?"

"Hmmm," said Possum, smoothing the black fur of his tail. "I'll be there, but I do hope I'm given a proper seat. Everyone should be able to see me and admire my tail. Don't you think I have a fine tail, Rabbit?" Saying this, Possum looked at Rabbit's little tuft of a tail and raised his eyebrow.

Rabbit felt anger boiling within him, but he pretended to be cheerful.

"Oh, yes," Rabbit said to Possum, "I'm sure you'll be given a seat of honor. And don't you think you should have your tail looking its very best for the occasion? Why don't I send someone over to trim and groom it for you?"

When Rabbit left Possum's lodge, he hurried over to see Cricket. Now Cricket was well known as a barber because he was such an expert cutter of hair.

"You must go to Possum's lodge tomorrow morning," Rabbit told Cricket.

Cricket made a face. "Not me!" he said. "I don't want to hear any more songs about beautiful tails!"

"There'll be no more songs," said Rabbit gleefully, "for I have a plan!" Then he whispered his secret in Cricket's ear. In a moment, Cricket smiled and nodded.

Early the next morning, Cricket set off for Possum's lodge. "Rabbit sent me," Cricket said. "I am here to prepare your glorious tail for the council meeting. Leave it to me, and I'll have your tail looking more lovely than ever!"

So Possum stretched out and dozed while Cricket worked on his tail. Cricket combed and fussed. Then he said, "I'll wind this red cord around your tail. It will keep the hairs nice and smooth until tonight's feast. You can untie it just before the dancing begins."

That night Possum arrived at the council meeting with his tail still tightly wrapped. When he was shown to the best seat, he sat down with a proud and happy smile on his face. Possum feasted with the other animals and talked over matters of importance with them. Then the drums began to beat. It was time for the dancing to begin.

Possum loosened the red cord from around his tail and stepped out onto the dance floor. He leaped high and swept low, singing all the while. "See my beautiful tail! See how I can raise it high! See what a fine color it is!"

Everyone shouted. "Oh, how they admire my tail!" Possum thought. He sang even louder. "See how thick and heavy my tail is! See how beautiful!"

The animals cheered him on. But then Possum heard laughing. Indeed, many of the animals were laughing so hard that tears were rolling down their cheeks. Some were holding their sides, and others were doubling over with laughter.

Possum stopped dancing. When he looked at his tail, his eyes opened wide in horror. His fine furry brush was gone. His tail was now as bald and scaly as a lizard's. There wasn't a hair on it. Cricket had snipped off every strand.

Possum was so embarrassed that he rolled over on his back and gave a silly grin. And that's just what possums do today when they're taken by surprise.

1. *Why was Rabbit jealous of Possum's tail?*

2. *What did Cricket secretly do while Possum was sleeping?*

3. *Do you think Possum got what he deserved? Why or why not?*

The Pleiades and the Pine

The Pleiades is a cluster of seven stars. Usually only six of them shine brightly enough to be seen.

Down through the centuries, people have used these stars to find their way at night. The earliest explorers plotted their courses by them. Today's sailors and pilots still do. This Cherokee story tells how the Pleiades came into being.

Boys sometimes used sticks and stones to play a game called *gatayusti*. They rolled the stones on the ground and then tried to strike them with long sticks. Once there were seven boys who spent all their time playing this game.

"Work in the fields!" said their fathers.

"Help harvest the corn!" said their mothers.

But the boys still took every chance they got to steal away and play gatayusti.

One day the mothers decided to teach their children a lesson. They gathered up the gatayusti stones and threw them into a pot to boil. When the boys came home for dinner, the mothers dished up bowls of stones instead of soup.

"You spend your time playing instead of working in the fields," they said. "You can eat stones instead of corn."

The boys grumbled and complained and then went off by themselves. When they didn't return, the mothers got worried and went out looking for them.

They found their sons behind the council house. The boys were dancing wildly and calling upon the spirits to help them. Round and round they whirled and leaped.

"Look!" one mother cried. "They aren't touching the ground!"

Sure enough, the boys' feet had left the earth. And with each circle they made, they rose higher into the air.

The women tried to grab their children, but it was too late. They couldn't reach them. One mother grabbed a gatayusti stick and managed to knock her son down. But the boy hit the ground so hard he sank into it. The earth closed over him.

The other six boys circled higher. At last they reached the sky. There they turned into the Pleiades. Those stars are also called *Anitsutsa,* which means "The Boys."

The six women watched the sky each night and wept for their sons. The seventh mother visited the spot where her son had sunken into the earth. Her tears watered the soil there until a little green sprout appeared. The sprout grew into the first pine tree. It held the spirit of this mother's son.

1. *How many stars are there in the Pleiades?*
2. *What did the mothers serve for dinner to punish their boys?*
3. *Where did the mothers find the boys when they didn't return?*

The Seven Sisters

The Ojibwa tell another story about the Pleiades. They say these seven stars are seven beautiful sisters.

One summer's evening a young man went fishing in a lake near his village. He was just about to push his canoe out into the water when a strange sound came to his ear. He stood very still and listened. Above the lapping of the water, he heard soft and beautiful singing.

The man turned his head this way and that but saw no one. Then, looking up, he saw a large basket floating down from the sky. The young man felt that this was something not meant for mortal eyes. He slipped quickly into the bushes and hid.

The basket came to rest on the shore of the lake. Seven young women stepped out of it. They were all beautiful. Long dark hair hung down the backs of their robes. They held hands in a circle and began to sway gently to the rhythm of their song. The young man had never seen anything so lovely. He stepped out from behind the bushes to join them in their dance.

The women turned toward him, their eyes wide with fright. Then they ran to the basket and climbed into it. Just before they rose into the sky, one of them looked directly into the young man's eyes. He felt as if his whole being was captured by that look. While all seven young women were beautiful, this one was by far the loveliest. The young man's heart was bursting with love as the basket disappeared upward.

All the next day the young man couldn't stop thinking about the beautiful woman. Sometimes he wondered if he'd really seen her. That evening, he went back to the lake.

The young man was not disappointed. Just as he hid behind a rock, he heard the sweet voices. Once more, the basket came down from the sky.

The seven young women stood timidly on the shore. "Do you think he'll return?" one of them asked.

"Are we safe here?" asked another.

"It's all right," said a third. "There's no one around. But hurry. Let us begin our dance. We must get home before sunset."

So the young women sang and danced again in a circle. While they did, the young man watched and waited. He had come up with a plan to catch his love.

When the woman he fancied was far from the basket, the young man leaped forward. He caught her by the arm and pulled her toward him. The other women screamed. They rushed for the basket, but the man held tight and wouldn't let go of the one young woman's arm.

"Come, sister!" the other women shouted. "Break free!" But the basket began to rise into the sky.

When it was out of sight, the young man released the young woman. She sank to the ground and buried her face in her hands. "Why have you done this to me?" she asked. "Why have you torn me from my sisters?"

"I mean you no harm," the young man cried. "I wish you only happiness. I . . . I have fallen in love with you."

The woman's heart softened. She thought he was sincere. She noticed, too, that he was quite handsome.

"But I can't remain on earth," she said. "My sisters and I are daughters of the Sun and Moon. We are the Pleiades." She pointed to the heavens. "I must go home!"

"Then I will go with you!" the young man said to her.

The Pleiades

"Oh, no!" she said. "My father, the Sun, would be very angry. We're forbidden to visit the earth. But this is such a beautiful place. We come here when our father is low in the sky and can't see us. He must not find out we've disobeyed him!"

But the man pleaded and begged. At last the young woman agreed to let him visit her home in the sky. "My sisters will return for me tomorrow evening. You can come home with me then," she said.

"I will speak to your father," the young man said. "I will tell him we're in love."

The two hid by the lake all the next day. Sure enough, in the evening the basket appeared in the sky. Six young women looked down anxiously, hoping to catch sight of their sister.

When the basket landed and the women saw the man, they shrank back in fear. But their sister told them she'd fallen in love. "This man," she announced, "shall come with me and be my husband."

The young man rode up to the sky in the basket. He soon found himself standing before the Sun.

"Why have you disobeyed me?" the angry Sun roared at his daughters. "Not only did you go to earth against my wishes, but now you've brought back a mortal!"

The young man stepped forward. He spoke openly of his love for the Sun's daughter. He talked of marriage. The young man's words went straight to the Sun's heart and softened it.

"I see that you truly love my daughter," said the Sun. "So I will allow you to remain here. But the disobedience will have to be punished. I banish *all* of you to the farthest part of the heavens. There you will live forever. And you must *never*, *ever* set foot on the earth again!"

The young man stepped forward. The daughter pulled him back and warned him to be still. But the young man was bold.

"Could my wife and I still go there sometimes?" he asked. "Couldn't we just visit? The earth is my home. I promise you we would return quickly."

"Oh, very well," the Sun growled. Actually, he admired this daring young man who was to be his son-in-law. "You and my daughter may visit earth now and then. But the rest of you," he said to his other daughters, "must never leave the sky!"

And so the sisters and the husband have lived ever since in a distant place in the heavens. Sometimes the husband and wife leave the sky and visit the earth. Then only six stars glow in the Pleiades.

1. *How is the Ojibwa story about the Pleiades similar to the Cherokee story?*

2. *Why did the seven young women only come to earth in the evening?*

3. *The young man's "heart was bursting," and the young woman's "heart softened." Does this mean they had heart trouble? If not, what does it mean?*

How Snakes Became Dangerous

> *Here are two stories that show respect for creatures often thought to be threatening. The word* bayous *in the first story refers to the marshy waterways found in the southern parts of the United States. Some of the snakes in the bayous possess deadly poison. But the Choctaws do not present them as evil villains. The Seminoles also view snakes as good creatures who only use their poison in defense.*

The First Poisonous Creatures
(A Choctaw Tale)

Long ago, a very poisonous vine grew along the edge of the bayous. Sometimes when the Choctaws bathed or swam there, they would brush up against it. The poison was strong enough to kill them, and it sometimes did.

Now the vine felt bad about this. He liked the Choctaws and didn't mean them any harm. But he had no way to warn them of his presence. At last he decided to rid himself of the poison.

The vine called together the chiefs of the snakes, bees, and wasps. "I want to give you my poison," he said. Until then, snakes, bees, and wasps had all been quite perfectly harmless.

The creatures discussed the vine's offer among themselves. At last they agreed to share the poison.

"I will take some," said the rattlesnake. "But before poisoning anyone, I will use the noise my tail makes as a warning. I will strike only if the warning is not heeded."

The bees and the wasps made similar promises. Before stinging anyone who disturbed them, they would warn the person by buzzing.

1. *What are bayous?*

2. *What gave snakes, wasps, and bees their poison?*

3. *How did the wasps and bees promise to warn someone before stinging?*

Why Snakes Can Bite (A Seminole Story)

Long ago rattlesnakes had no fangs. They were completely harmless.

Then one day a warrior came across a mother rattlesnake and her nest of babies. He killed the babies and cut off their tails. The mother escaped.

Rattlesnake and her children.

For three days, the mother cried and mourned for her lost children. Then she went to the village chief.

"One of your warriors has killed my babies," she said. "I had absolutely no way to defend them."

The chief made the rattlesnake a set of fangs and fitted them into her mouth.

"The next time a man bothers you," he said, "you can bite him."

Since that time, the Seminoles have refused to kill rattlesnakes. They know that the snakes won't bite if they're left undisturbed.

4. *Who killed the mother rattlesnake's babies?*

5. *What did the mother rattlesnake do about it?*

6. *Who gave the rattlesnake fangs?*

The Formation of Multnomah Falls

In northwestern Oregon there is a beautiful waterfall that drops from a cliff to a misty pond below. This Multnomah story explains its beginnings.

There once was a chief of the Multnomah people who had a most lovely daughter. Everyone in the tribe admired her beauty and her kindness. She made children laugh and old people smile.

This young woman's father wanted to find her a worthy husband. So he chose a handsome warrior from his neighbors, the Clatsop people. The young man and woman met, and soon they fell in love.

It took many days to prepare a proper wedding celebration. There was food to be cooked. There were swimming and canoe races on the Columbia River to be planned. Everyone joined in the preparations.

But before the wedding was to take place, a terrible sickness swept through the tribe. Children were the first to die. Soon, however, even strong warriors fell to the disease. Plans for the marriage were put aside as the village became filled with pain and suffering.

The chief called together his council of wise men and warriors. "Is the Great Spirit angry with us?" he asked.

But no one had an answer. The Multnomah continued to die.

Then a very old man came into the village. He sat before the chief and his council and spoke in a whisper. "I have been in the mountains for many summers and many winters," he said. "Long ago, when I was young, my father told me a secret. He was a great Multnomah medicine man. I have kept his secret until now.

"My father told me that when I became old, the Great Spirit would send a sickness upon our people. There would be no cure. All would die unless a sacrifice was made to him."

"What does the Great Spirit want?" the chief asked.

"A pure and innocent maiden must willingly give her life for her people," the man said. "She must be the daughter of a present or past chief."

The chief's face paled, but he didn't say a word or move a muscle. The old man continued speaking.

"She must go by herself to the top of a high cliff. Then she must throw herself onto the rocks below. If she does, the sickness will leave at once."

The chief was silent for a long time. At last he turned to his council and said, "Call together all the maidens whose fathers and grandfathers have been chiefs. Bring them to me at once."

A dozen young women came before the village council. Among them was the chief's own daughter. He told them what the old man had said. "I believe his words are true," the chief said. Then he fell silent. Moments later he shook his head. "No!" he said. "I cannot ask any of you to sacrifice yourself. This meeting is ended!"

The sickness stayed in the village. More people died. The chief's daughter became filled with sorrow. She who loved laughter and joy felt deeply the pain and suffering around her. "Is it in my power," she wondered, "to put an end to the sickness and death? Should I sacrifice myself to save my people?" But she was young and in love and wanted to go on living.

A few days later, her young Clatsop warrior fell ill. He was flushed with fever. The young woman knew he would be next to die. She had to do something.

In the morning, she slipped silently away from the village. She traveled through the forest all day and at sunset she reached the edge of a high cliff. The woman looked down at the rocks below. There was a stream there that led to a river. The woman stared at the rocks. Then she turned her face upward and lifted her arms.

"Oh, Great Spirit," she cried, "will you end the suffering if I give my life? I need strength. I need to know my death will save my people. If you will accept me as a sacrifice, show me some sign."

Just then the moon rose over the forest. The woman closed her eyes, folded her arms across her chest, and jumped.

Next morning, everyone in the village arose from their beds feeling healthy and fit. The sickness was gone. The people gloried in their good health. They hugged each other and laughed and sang.

Then someone asked, "But how did our good fortune come to be? Could one of the maidens have been sacrificed?"

The chief felt his blood run cold. Quickly he called the daughters and granddaughters before him. Eleven appeared. His own daughter was missing.

The chief and the young Clatsop warrior hurried along the trail that led to the cliff. The others followed. At the foot of the cliff, the warrior found his love, the sweet daughter of the Multnomah chief. Her people buried her there.

The chief prayed over his daughter's grave. "Oh, Great Spirit, does my daughter rest easy in the land of the spirits? I must know she is happy. Show me a sign."

Just then the sound of rushing water came from above. The people looked up and saw a silvery ribbon pour over the top of the cliff. It fell as the maiden had and broke into a mist.

To this day, water tumbles from that cliff into a pool below. Sometimes, especially at sunset, the spirit of the maiden comes back to see the waterfall. She stands to the side of Multnomah Falls, wrapped in mist.

1. *Why were the wedding plans put aside?*

2. *What finally made the chief's daughter decide to sacrifice herself?*

3. *What sign showed the chief his daughter was happy?*

How the Narwhal Got Its Tusk

The narwhal is a large animal that swims in the northern seas. This tale explains the origin of the male narwhal's long twisted tusk.

The Greedy Grandmother

Long ago, an old woman and her two grandchildren lived at the edge of a village. Visitors seldom came to their hut. The grandson, who had been blind since birth, and the granddaughter were very lonely.

One day the old woman said, "We must go on a journey." Without telling anyone where they were headed, the three of them set out on foot.

After traveling for several days, they were caught in a swirling snowstorm. Luckily, they found an empty igloo and took shelter in it. They were warm and dry, but they had no food.

They grew weaker and weaker while waiting for the snow to stop. "We're starving!" the granddaughter cried.

And then one day a fat bear came to the igloo. "Quick," the grandmother said to her grandson. "It's a bear. You must shoot him."

"But I cannot see him," the boy said.

"I'll aim the arrow," the grandmother said. "But you're stronger than I am. You must pull the bow string."

The old woman led the boy outside. She aimed the arrow. The boy shot. He heard a loud thud.

"You missed the bear!" the grandmother cried. "The arrow struck the wall. What a shame!" Then the old woman turned and whispered to her granddaughter. "Don't tell him he hit the bear. Then we won't have to give him any of the meat. There'll be more for us. Let's drag the bear away and eat the meat in secret!"

The grandson heard them boil the meat. He smelled it cooking.

The grandmother and granddaughter had a fine meal. They ate and ate. But the granddaughter let some of the meat fall from her mouth and roll under her collar.

At last the grandmother was stuffed full of bear meat. She fell asleep, and the girl went to her brother. She reached down her collar and got out the pieces of meat. He ate them quickly.

"I'm thirsty," the boy said. "Please lead me to the lake."

When they had reached the lake, the boy

said, "You had better go now, Sister. Grandmother will awaken soon. But leave a track of stones so I can feel my way back to you."

The girl returned to the igloo while her brother remained by the water.

1. *Why did the grandmother aim the arrow for her grandson?*

2. *How did the boy know he had killed the bear?*

3. *Why did the granddaughter let some pieces of meat roll under her collar?*

The Magic of Sight

Soon a large bird came down and landed beside the boy.

"Hang on to my neck," the bird said.

The boy grabbed hold, and the bird dove into the lake. Deep underwater they went. The boy was frightened at first, but then he realized he wasn't feeling the water's chill. And he could breathe!

At last the bird returned to the surface. "How do you feel?" he asked the boy.

"Wonderful! I think I'm beginning to see!"

The bird took the boy underwater again and again. Each time they came up, the boy's vision was clearer. After the fourth dive, the boy exclaimed, "I can see everything now!"

The boy saw the stones his sister had left. He followed them back to the igloo. There he saw a big bear skin stretched out on the ground.

He walked into the igloo and asked his grandmother where the skin had come from.

"Oh, that," she said. "Some traders came by while you were away. They gave us some bear meat and left the skin behind. Good luck, eh?"

4. *What took the boy underwater?*

5. *What did the boy realize after the fourth time they had dived?*

6. *Where did the grandmother say the bear skin had come from?*

A Whaling Trip

The three stayed in the igloo until the bad weather had passed. Then, since the boy could see, his grandmother put him to work. They journeyed to the ocean, where whales swam close to shore.

The boy prepared to harpoon a whale. He tied the end of one line to his sister's leg. This meant she was his partner. When he'd killed the whale, she would get the same amount of meat as he would.

"Tie me, too!" the grandmother said. So the boy tied his grandmother's leg to the end of another line.

First the boy harpooned a small whale. His sister grinned.

"Get one for me!" the grandmother shouted to the boy.

So he harpooned a whale with the grandmother's line. The whale was a large one that had been swimming further out. But it was only wounded. The whale dragged the grandmother toward the water.

"Help me!" she screamed.

The old woman went into the water and was dragged under.

But she came up again. "Toss me my knife!" she cried. "So I can cut myself free!"

Just at that moment, a whirlpool caught the woman and spun her round and round. Her long hair twirled into a thick tight braid. The big whale dragged, the whirlpool pulled, and the woman disappeared suddenly from sight.

At the bottom of the sea, the woman turned into a male narwhal. Her braided hair became a long twisted tooth that stuck

Male narwhal

out from its jaw. And this is how the male narwhal got its tusk.

7. *What did the boy's tying the harpoon line to his sister's leg mean?*

8. *Why was the grandmother's whale able to drag her out to sea?*

9. *What part of the grandmother's body became the narwhal's tusk?*

How the Winds Began to Blow

In this happy tale, Igaluk, the Moon Spirit, brings good fortune to a lonely couple.

The Dream

When the world was new, there were no winds. When it rained, the water poured straight down from the sky. The snow never drifted, and the trees never whispered to one another. All was quiet and calm.

A certain couple lived at that time in a little village near the mouth of the Yukon River. This couple had no children, and they were quite lonely. They often imagined how rich their lives would be if only they had a child to love.

Each evening, the man and woman curled up near their fire. They held each other close and wished for a son or daughter. Then one night, the woman had a strange vision. In a dream she saw a sled being pulled by three dogs. One dog was brown, one white, and one black. The sled drew up in front of her house, and its driver beckoned silently to her.

The woman climbed upon the sled. The driver cracked his whip, and they were off.

At first the runners skimmed over the icy ground. As the sled gained speed, it rose into the air and raced among the stars. Then the woman knew that the driver had to be Igaluk, the Moon Spirit. The woman was happy, for Igaluk brought good fortune to those who were sad and lonely.

The woman enjoyed her ride in the sky and felt rather sorry when the sled descended. It set down upon a wide field of ice. The field was bare of everything but a single tree.

Igaluk pointed to the tree and said, "I know you have wished for a child. If you make a doll from the trunk of that tree, you will find happiness."

Then the woman woke up.

1. What did the couple wish for?

2. What was the name of the spirit in the woman's dream?

3. What did the spirit tell the woman to do to find happiness?

The Doll

It was still dark, but the woman shook her husband until he awoke. She told him her dream and asked him to find the tree.

"It was only a dream," he said. "Now go back to sleep!"

But the woman begged and pleaded. Her husband knew he wouldn't get a good night's sleep again until he found that tree. Just before dawn, he shouldered his axe and set off into the cold outside.

The man trudged through the snow until he came to the edge of the village. "With all the work I have to do," he grumbled, "here I am chasing a dream!"

But a strange sight stopped his grumbling. A bright silvery light stretched out before him. The path was shining like a moonbeam.

The man followed the path for several hours. Then he found a single tree glowing in a circle of light. He knew it was the tree his wife had seen in her dream. He cut it down with his axe and carried it home.

That evening the man carved the figure of a boy from the wood. His wife made a sealskin suit and dressed the figure. Then she set it on a bench near the door. The man carved a set of tiny dishes, which his wife filled with food and water. She set them down before the doll.

"Are we being silly?" she shyly asked her husband.

"Perhaps we're fools," he said. "Surely nothing will come of this."

The couple went to bed in a gloomy mood. But during the night the woman heard a strange noise. Something was moving inside their house. "It's the doll!" she cried, waking her husband. Sure enough, the doll had eaten the food and drunk the water. It seemed quite alive.

The couple hugged the doll. They cuddled him and played with him for hours until they grew very tired. Then they made him a little bed and went back to sleep with smiles on their faces.

In the morning, however, the doll had disappeared.

The couple rushed from their house to search for him. But the doll was nowhere to be found. They returned home sadder and more lonely than ever.

4. *Why didn't the man want to go out?*

5. *What was in the circle of light the man found at the end of the path?*

6. *What happened to the couple's doll during the night?*

The Winds

The doll was excited with his new life and decided he must see the world. He followed the same bright path the man had taken and traveled quickly to the eastern edge of day. There the sky met the earth and walled in the light. And there the doll saw a hole in the wall of sky. It was covered by a flap of animal skin. The cover was bulging, as if a strong force were pushing on it from the other side. The doll was curious, and he pulled back the flap.

Whoosh! Whoosh! A great wind rushed in. It carried with it birds and animals. The doll peered through the hole and saw that the Sky Land on the other side looked just like the earth. It had trees, mountains, and rivers.

When he felt the wind had blown long enough, he placed the skin back over the hole. He said sternly, "Wind, blow hard sometimes. Blow softly sometimes. And sometimes, don't blow at all." Then he went on his way.

In time, he came to the southern edge of day. There he saw another piece of skin covering a hole. Again, he was curious and drew back the covering.

Whoosh! Winds poured in from the Sky Land. These were warmer winds, and they too brought birds and animals. After a time, the doll closed up the opening. He gave the southern winds the same command he'd given those from the east.

The doll found another opening in the sky wall when he arrived in the west. When he uncovered this hole, the westerly winds brought in rain and ocean spray. He covered the hole quite quickly and gave the western winds his instructions.

When the doll came to the north, he let in some icy cold winds. They brought snow and sleet. They froze the little doll so that he could barely move. He pulled the skin cover over the hole and shut out the storm. Once more, he gave the northern winds the same command. "Wind, blow hard sometimes. Blow softly sometimes. And sometimes, don't blow at all."

By now the doll was weary of traveling. He was satisfied that he'd seen the world. He decided to go back to the village and the people who had treated him so kindly.

When the doll returned, the couple was overjoyed. They listened as he told of his travels and explained how he'd let in the winds. Word spread among the villagers.

And soon, the winds began to blow. Some days they blew hard. Some days they blew softly, and some days were still and calm. The people were happy, for the winds brought birds and animals. And they brought good hunting.

The couple held a feast to honor Igaluk, the Moon Spirit, who had given them such good fortune. And since that time, people have made dolls for their children. They know that dolls bring happiness to those who care for them.

7. *What did the wind bring to the villagers?*

8. *From which direction did the coldest winds come?*

9. *Where did the doll go after he had finished his travels?*

The Star Woman

The Apinaye of Brazil told of a time when heaven sent many gifts to earth. The acts of a disloyal husband changed this.

Once there was a young man who had a beautiful wife. But not long after they were married, the woman fell sick and died. The man became very sad and could not sleep at night. So he would lie outside on the leaf of a bacaba palm, staring up at the stars in the sky.

One warm night he caught sight of an especially bright star. The man watched it sparkle for a long time. Suddenly the star fell to earth. It landed beside him and changed into a beautiful woman. She was small and slender.

"Move over a little," the woman said. "Let me lie beside you, and we can talk."

They talked all night, and at dawn the woman returned to the heavens.

Every night for five nights, the Star Woman came down to visit the young man. Each night he found her more lovely. She eased his loneliness. For the first time since his wife's death, the man felt happy. "Will you stay with me?" he asked.

The Star Woman said she would. So the man took her into his house and put her in a large gourd. After that, whenever he wanted, the man would open the gourd and talk to her.

One day while the man was away, his sister decided to surprise him by cleaning his house.

"What is this?" she exclaimed when she saw the big gourd. She looked inside and discovered the Star Woman.

She scolded the young man when he returned. "Brother," she said, "you cannot keep this woman hidden in your house! You must ask her to be your wife!"

So a proper wedding was held.

"Now that we're married," the Star Woman said to her husband, "please make me a garden plot."

"A what?" the man asked. At that time, no one had ever heard of a garden. People ate only rotten wood, leaves, roots, and wild coconuts.

"Wait here," the Star Woman said. She threw a cotton thread to the sky and climbed up it. Soon she returned with as many yams and potatoes as she could carry.

"Try these," she said to her husband.

"Oh, no!" he answered fearfully, for he had never seen such things. He was afraid they might make him sick. But his wife held his head and forced him to eat. The man didn't get the least bit sick. In fact he felt fine. And the food tasted wonderful.

The man told other people about the new foods. He also prepared a garden plot. And when the plot was ready, his wife went to the sky and brought back more things. She brought corn, rice, beans, peanuts, and the other foods that are grown today. They all went into the garden.

But the husband wasn't faithful to his wife. Even as the crops were growing, he was falling in love with another woman.

The Star Woman found out about her husband's disloyalty. She was hurt and angry, and she rose back into the sky. This time she didn't come back. If her husband had been true, she would have continued to bring gifts from heaven to earth. But he wasn't, and so the people never received all that there is in heaven.

1. *How did the Star Woman first come down to earth?*

2. *Who found the Star Woman hidden in the gourd?*

3. *What did people eat before the Star Woman came?*

Rabbit the Trickster

Many of the world's mythologies include tales of tricks and pranks. The trickster is a clever character who breaks rules and usually gets what he wants. In Native American mythology, the identity of the trickster varies from region to region. On the North American plains, stories of Coyote are told. In the northwest and far north, Raven was the trickster. Rabbit was the major trickster of the southwest. The trickster is both a rascal and a hero.

Rabbit was very unhappy. He felt he wasn't as strong or as well-equipped for life as the other animals. So he went to talk to Master-of-Breath, the Life Controller.

"All the other animals have ways to protect themselves," Rabbit said. "When I'm attacked, I can only run. It's not fair!"

"Do these tasks for me," said Master-of-Breath, "and I will give you new powers. First, bring Rattlesnake to me."

So Rabbit picked up a long stick and went looking for Rattlesnake. When he found him, Rattlesnake was coiled and ready to strike. Rabbit approached him and said,

"Master-of-Breath has asked me to find out how long you are. If you'll get out of your coil, I'll measure you."

Now Rattlesnake loved nothing more than showing off his great length. So he uncoiled and stretched out before Rabbit. Then Rabbit ran the point of his stick right through Rattlesnake's head and killed him. Rabbit carried the dead snake back to Master-of-Breath.

"Well done," said the Master. "Now go bring me that swarm of gnats you see flying in the air."

Rabbit took a bag and went to sit beneath the swarm. "Hello!" he cried to the King of the Gnats. "Master-of-Breath has asked me to count your band. He cannot believe it is as large as it looks!"

The King of the Gnats was very proud of his large band of followers. He was quite willing to let them be counted.

"Fly into the bag," said Rabbit, "and I shall count you as you enter."

The king entered the bag, and so did all the others. Rabbit tied up the bag and carried it back to the Master.

Master-of-Breath said to Rabbit, "Look at what you've done with the powers you already possess. You don't need more to get

Rabbit tricks the gnats

along in this life. Go now and use what you already have."

1. *What did Rabbit complain about to Master-of-Breath?*
2. *How did Rabbit trick Rattlesnake?*
3. *What powers did Rabbit find out he already had?*

How Coyote Got His Cunning

The trickster often relies on cleverness to make up for a lack of something else. This Karok tale explains how Coyote got his cunning.

The great god Kareya created all the world. He made the animals, and he made a man. Kareya gave the man the most power. He gave each animal an equal amount of power.

But then Kareya decided to change this. So he went to the man and said, "Make as many bows and arrows as there are kinds of animals. Give the longest bow and arrow to the one that should have the most power. Give the shortest to the one that should have the least."

So the man made many bows and arrows. When they were ready, Kareya called the animals together and explained his plan. He told them that in the morning, the man would pass out the bows and arrows.

When Coyote heard this, he immediately began to plot.

"If I stay awake all night," he decided, "I'll be first in line in the morning. Surely the man will give the longest bow and arrow to whoever's first in line."

So when the other animals went to sleep, Coyote stayed up. He sang and whistled to himself in the dark. But by midnight Coyote was feeling very sleepy. He jumped up and down to keep himself awake. But the noise woke the other animals, and he had to stop.

At last Coyote was so sleepy he couldn't keep his eyes open. He took two small sticks and sharpened their ends. He used them to prop open his eyelids.

But even with his eyes held open by the sticks, Coyote couldn't stay awake. Soon he'd fallen asleep and was snoring. The sharp sticks pierced his eyelids. Then, instead of holding them open, the sticks kept his eyelids closed. In the morning, the other animals got up fresh and rested. Coyote slept on and on.

The animals went to the man and received their bows and arrows. Cougar was given the longest. Bear got the next longest. The last bow and arrow were given to Frog.

"But wait!" said the man. "I still have the shortest bow and arrow to give out. Who have I missed?"

Then the animals and the man heard snoring. They looked around and saw Coyote fast asleep.

The man pulled the sticks from Coyote's eyelids and handed him the shortest bow and arrow. The other animals laughed and laughed. But the man began to feel sorry for Coyote, who would be weakest of them all. He prayed to Kareya for help. In answer, Kareya gave Coyote more cunning than anyone else.

1. *Which animal was supposed to get the longest bow and arrow? The shortest?*
2. *Why did Coyote get the shortest?*
3. *How did Kareya help Coyote?*

Coyote Tricks the Trader

When white settlers moved west across North America, they often took advantage of the people who lived there. Here is a story in which Coyote turns things around a bit.

Once there was a white man who believed he was a very sharp trader. "Nobody gets the best of me!" he was often heard to say. This fellow used every cheating trick you could think of to get himself a good deal. Many people would have been happy to see his downfall.

"I think I know someone who can out-cheat you!" the trader was told one day.

"That can't be!" the white man exclaimed. "I've had this trading post for years. I've cheated everyone around here."

Indeed, the white man continued to do well. He cheated and tricked, and the goods in his post kept piling higher. But then one afternoon he met up with Coyote, and everything changed.

Coyote sat down in the sun in front of the trading post. "There's the one who can outsmart you!" someone said to the trader.

The white man looked at Coyote and didn't think much of him. "He doesn't look so tricky," the trader said.

He strutted over to Coyote. "Hey," he said, "I hear you're a clever dealer. Let's see you outsmart me!"

"I'm sorry," Coyote said. "I'd like to give it a try. But I don't have my cheating medicine with me."

"Cheating medicine!" the trader exclaimed. "That's quite an excuse! Well then, go get it."

"I live a long ways from here," said Coyote. "It would take me too long to walk home. But if you loan me your horse, I'll be happy to go."

"All right, you can borrow my horse. Go home and get your cheating medicine." The white man laughed. He was sure he was calling Coyote's bluff.

"You know," said Coyote, "your horse seems afraid of me. He might throw me when I try to ride him. Why don't you loan me your clothes? Then your horse will think I'm you."

The trader gave Coyote every piece of his clothing. "There now, go get your cheating medicine—if there is such a thing! If not, admit you're a fool!"

Sly Coyote

So Coyote rode off. And the trader stood naked in the dust. He stared at Coyote—and at his horse and his clothes—disappearing across the plains.

1. *What was the trader best known for?*
2. *What did Coyote say he didn't have with him?*
3. *What did Coyote take from the trader?*

Raven Steals a Lake

Many northern myths picture Raven as the creator. But he is also described as a greedy trickster. Sometimes he disguises himself as a handsome man and tries to marry beautiful young women. Sometimes, as in this Haida tale, Raven tricks his fellow animals.

One day Raven decided to explore the Queen Charlotte Islands. So he left the mainland, flew over the water, and landed in a forest there. As he was walking and exploring the area, Raven heard voices. He peered through the bushes and saw four beavers in a clearing. They were playing a gambling game called *lahal*.

"I win!" Raven heard one beaver shout. The beaver had just guessed which of several marked sticks the other beavers were holding.

Raven was hungry by now, and all he could think of was food. The beavers were plump, and they looked happy. Raven was sure they'd been eating well.

Now he could have simply asked them for something to eat. But that wasn't

Raven's way. He thought it would be much better to cheat them out of a meal. So Raven turned himself into a little old man and hobbled into the clearing.

"Ah, cousins!" he said. "I have found you at last. My father told me to seek you out if I were ever in need. He told me you'd take care of me."

The beavers were quite surprised to hear this human calling himself their cousin. But fast-talking Raven convinced them that they really were related. So the beavers welcomed Raven and suggested he come home with them.

"Sit by the fire," the beavers told Raven when they got to their lodge. Then one of them disappeared through a back doorway and returned with a large salmon. Raven noticed that the beaver's legs were wet and that the fish was very fresh.

Raven had never eaten salmon before. It tasted wonderful. He decided to find out what was beyond the back door.

Next morning the beavers gathered up their gambling sticks. "We're going to the far side of the island to play lahal with some other beavers," they said. "Come join us."

But the old man who was Raven shook his grizzled head. "I am old," he said. "It takes me a long time to recover from a journey. I think I'll just rest today."

"Would you like one of us to stay with you?" the beavers asked. "Oh, no," said Raven. "Don't spoil your day on my account. Go play your game."

As soon as the beavers were out of sight, Raven hurried through the back door of the lodge. There before him was a large clear lake. Lots of fat salmon were jumping and splashing in the water. Raven waded right in. There were so many fish he could scoop them up in his hands. Raven ate one, and then another. "Why, they're delicious!" he said. "Just delicious!"

By the time the beavers came home that night, Raven was back in the lodge. He was full of salmon and napping happily. The beavers let their guest sleep.

The next day, the beavers went off again to play lahal. Once more, Raven went to the lake and ate his fill. As he munched on salmon, he thought, "It doesn't seem fair that the beavers keep all this to themselves. Soon I must be off. But how can I leave these tasty fish behind?"

So Raven decided to steal the beavers' lake. It wasn't hard. He simply rolled it up like a blanket. He tucked in the edges so that no water would spill out. Then he changed back into a bird and flew up into the air. But he didn't go far.

Raven settled in the boughs of a pine tree and waited for the beavers to return. Being who he was, he wanted to get a good laugh out of the situation.

"Where has our guest gone?" the beavers asked when they returned and found their home empty. Then they heard a shout from the back of the lodge. One of the beavers had just discovered that the lake and the salmon were missing.

They searched all over and didn't stop until they heard laughter. It was coming from above. The beavers looked up and saw Raven clutching the lake.

"Thief!" one of them shouted. "Give us back our lake."

Raven held the lake tightly in his claws and laughed even harder.

"Get him!" cried one of the beavers, and they all attacked the tree. They gnawed at it with their teeth until it swayed and crashed to the ground. But Raven just flew to another pine. Again the beavers chewed down the tree. Again Raven flew to another. He teased the beavers and laughed at them as they got angrier and angrier.

Finally Raven grew tired of this sport. He shouted, "Farewell!" and flew off for the mainland with the lake in his beak.

"After him!" cried the beavers. They weren't going to give up their lake and salmon so easily.

Raven flew along the coast looking for a good place to put down the lake. Here and there he spilled drops of water. These became the rivers of the mainland. Sometimes salmon fell out with the water, and they made their homes in the rivers.

Raven at last found a peaceful and pleasant valley, and there he laid the lake. By then it was a bit smaller than it had been. But it was still quite fine and still held many fish. Raven looked at it proudly. "Now there's salmon for everyone," he said. "Especially me!"

And what of the beavers? Well, they didn't give up. Although their journey was hard, they followed Raven all the way to the peaceful valley. But unlike Raven, they had no magical powers. They couldn't steal back their lake. The best they could do was make a new home beside it.

The beavers never returned to the islands. And that's why today many beavers are found on the mainland but none on the Queen Charlotte islands.

1. *How did Raven disguise himself to fool the beavers?*
2. *What did the beavers give Raven to eat?*
3. *How did Raven steal the beaver's lake?*

The Animals Get Angry

Native American mythology shows great respect for nature. It shows us that all things are parts of a whole. Native Americans described themselves as brothers and sisters of the earth, and of the animals and plants that grow upon it. They celebrated the universe and everything within it.

This story tells how the Cherokees learned to respect the creatures of the earth.

In the early days, when all was as it should be, animals, fish, insects, and plants could talk. They lived with people in harmony and peace. But as time went on, the people forgot that these beings were members of their own family. The people invented bows and arrows as well as knives, spears, and hooks. They began killing the creatures. Finally the creatures decided to protect themselves.

They called a big council meeting. Little Deer, chief of all the deer and their swiftest messenger, spoke first.

"We have to show the humans that they must not kill creatures thoughtlessly.

We'll tell them we are going to bring disease to every hunter who does not ask pardon when he kills one of us."

So they sent word to the nearest settlement. They told the people that when a deer was slain, the hunter had to say a prayer and ask the deer's pardon.

"When a deer is shot," they said, "Little Deer will run swiftly to the place where it happened. He will bend over the deer and ask his spirit if the hunter prayed for pardon. If the answer is yes, all is well. If the answer is no, Little Deer will enter the hunter's cabin invisibly and strike the hunter with disease. The hunter will become weak and helpless."

After this message was sent, the snakes and the fish came up with other ideas. "We'll make those who kill recklessly dream about snakes wrapping themselves around and around them," said a rattlesnake. "Their throats will tighten and they'll choke to death in their sleep."

"We'll make them dream of eating rotten fish," said a minnow. "Their own thoughts will make them so sick they'll die."

"Stop!" the plants cried. "You're as wicked as the humans. Your plots will never encourage friendship. Instead of attacking them, we plants shall help the humans when they call on us in their need."

And that is how medicine came into the world. Each plant has its use. Plants offer remedies to cure the diseases brought about by the thoughtless people and the angry animals. Even weeds were made for good purposes. The medicine man knows which medicine to use for a sick person because the spirit of the plant tells him.

1. *Why were the animals angry?*

2. *What was the snakes' idea for punishing the hunters?*

3. *Where did medicine come from?*

Lost Lake

The animal world and the human world are closely related. The hero of this Wasco legend looks to an elk as his guardian and teacher.

Under the shadow of Mount Hood, the Wasco people fished peacefully in the Columbia River. They hunted in thick forests of tall firs. Among these people lived a young hunter named Plain Feather. The spirit of a great elk watched over Plain Feather and taught him where to look for game. With the great elk as his guardian spirit, Plain Feather became the best hunter in his tribe.

"Never kill more than you can use," the guardian spirit cautioned Plain Feather. "Kill only for your present needs."

Plain Feather followed the spirit's advice and killed only for food. Many of the other hunters shot animals for sport. Sometimes they left the bodies to rot in the forest.

Smart Crow, another young Wasco hunter, was jealous of Plain Feather's skills. So he came up with a plan to make Plain Feather disobey the great elk.

Smart Crow pretended he had had a vision. "The spirits spoke to me," he said. "They told me a bad winter is coming. We must kill all the animals we can and store their meat for the days ahead."

The other hunters believed Smart Crow. They went into the woods and hunted down many of the animals.

At first Plain Feather wouldn't go with them. "I won't kill any more than I can eat," he said firmly.

"You're a disgrace!" Smart Crow shouted for all to hear. "You're the most skillful hunter among us, yet you're ready to let your people starve!"

Plain Feather loved his people and didn't want them to suffer. At last he decided to go hunting along the Hood River. Plain Feather killed deer and bears. Then he came upon a huge herd of elk. He killed all but one of them. This elk was wounded, and it escaped into the forest.

Plain Feather followed the wounded elk, not knowing it was his own guardian spirit. He tracked it through the forest and up into the mountains until he came to a beautiful lake. There he found the elk lying in the water not far from shore.

Hunting the elk

Plain Feather waded in but then began to sink. The elk sank, too. They both went down to the bottom of the lake. Plain Feather couldn't fight his way back to the surface. He could, however, still breathe.

The water at the lake bottom was clear. Surrounding Plain Feather were the shapes of what looked like human beings. But these were the spirits of the many deer, bear, and elk he had killed.

"Draw him in," a deep voice whispered. Plain Feather was pulled closer to the wounded elk. "Draw him in," the strange voice said again. At last Plain Feather was right beside his guardian spirit.

"Why did you disobey me?" the great elk asked. "I told you to never kill more than you needed. Yet here are the spirits of all the animals you've slain." Then he said sadly, "I can no longer be your guardian."

The voice sadly whispered one last time. "Cast him out," the great elk said. The spirits cast Plain Feather out of the water. He found himself on the shore of the lake, wet and shivering.

With his head down and his heart heavy, Plain Feather made his way back to the village. He went into his tent and pulled his blanket around him.

"What's wrong?" the villagers asked.

"I am sick," Plain Feather answered. "I have lost my guardian spirit. He is in the lake of the lost spirits." Then Plain Feather lay back and died. Since that time, the lake in the mountains has been known as Lost Lake.

1. *What did the great elk warn Plain Feather about?*

2. *Why did Plain Feather decide to start killing many animals?*

3. *What did Plain Feather lose?*

The Last Buffalo

This Kiowa story tells of the slaughter of vast herds of buffalo. It contains both history and myth.

The Kiowas depended on the buffalo for life itself. They made their clothes and moccasins from its hide. They ate its meat. They made water containers from the buffalo's skin and stomach.

The buffalo also played an important role in the Kiowa religion. Priests used parts of the buffalo when they said prayers for healing. A buffalo calf was sacrificed during the sun dance.

The Kiowas honored the buffalo over all other animals. And the buffalo loved the Kiowas in return. One day white people came and tried to build railroads across Kiowa land. Then the buffalo protected the Kiowas. They tore up the railroad tracks and chased the white settlers' cattle and horses from the ranges.

The whites made war on the buffalo. They hired hunters to do nothing but kill buffalo. These hunters were paid by

The last buffalo

the number of animals they shot. They sometimes killed one hundred buffalo in a single day.

The buffalo could see that their end was near. No longer could they share the earth with the Kiowa people. Their time had come.

Early one morning a young Kiowa woman stood alone ouside her tent. The sun was coming up on the other side of Medicine Creek. Through the mist rising from the water, the woman saw a vision. It was the last buffalo herd.

The herd's leader walked toward Mount Scott. The cows, calves, and bulls who still lived followed him. As the woman watched, the face of the mountain opened.

Inside Mount Scott was another world. It was fresh and green. The only sound that came from it was the music made by the birds and the wind. There was no booming of guns. The last buffalo walked into this world of peace and beauty. Then the mountain closed, and the herd disappeared.

1. *What did the Kiowas make from the buffalo's stomach?*

2. *Why did the whites make war on the buffalo?*

3. *Where did the last buffalo herd go?*

The Three Worlds

The Creating Power wanted all beings to live in peace and harmony. As this story warns, we must not take for granted the earth and its creatures.

There was a world before this world. But the Creating Power was not pleased with the way things were going. Human beings had forgotten how to live in harmony with other creatures. They were needlessly slaying animals. They were forgetting their prayers of thanks for the bounties of the earth. And they were arguing among themselves over patches of land.

"I will put an end to this," said the Creating Power, "and make a new world."

He lit the sacred pipe and fanned its sparks until the whole world burst into flames. When every single creature was charred and burned, the Creating Power made new ones from their ashes. But the human beings in this new world didn't act human. They argued and fought over land, water, and food. They murdered each other, and they murdered the animals.

So the Creating Power said to himself, "I will sing three songs to bring down heavy rains. Then I'll sing a fourth song to crack open the earth and bring up more water."

The Creating Power sang his songs, and soon everything was covered with water. The Creating Power floated on his sacred pipe for a long time, drifting with the winds. At last the rain stopped. The people and animals had all drowned.

A single turtle remained alive. It swam in the water behind the Creating Power. Now the turtle is known for its strength and its ability to survive. The turtle's heart is great medicine. It keeps beating for a long time after the turtle is dead.

"Dive deep down under the water," the Creating Power told the turtle. "Bring up some mud from the bottom."

The turtle dove under the water and was gone a long time. The Creating Power began to wonder if he had drowned. But at last the turtle returned to the surface. "I got to the bottom!" he sputtered. "I brought back some earth!" Sure enough, the turtle's shell was smeared with mud.

The Creating Power scraped the mud from the turtle's shell. He molded and shaped it. The mud began to grow. Soon the

Creating Power was able to stand on dry land. Then he waved his pipe and commanded the land to spread. It grew and grew until it replaced all the water.

"Oh, no!" the Creating Power said. "Too much water is bad, but some water is very necessary." The Creating Power cried, and his tears became oceans, lakes, rivers, and streams.

Then the Creating Power waved his pipe again, and the bodies of animals, birds, and plants appeared on the land. He stamped on the earth, and they came alive.

Next the Creating Power took some of the earth and molded it into the shape of men and women. He used red earth and white earth and black earth and yellow earth. He stamped on the ground, and the people came alive.

The Creating Power spoke to all the new people. "Listen," he said. "In the first world I made, the people were bad. So I burned it up. The creatures of the second world were bad, too. I drowned them. This is the third world I have made. Look! I have created a rainbow for you as a sign that no more floods will come.

"Now you must live in peace with one another and with other living things.

You who are red, white, black, and yellow must live as brothers and sisters. You must live side by side with the animals who walk, fly, and crawl, and with the plants that grow from the earth. If you do this, all will be well. But if you make this world ugly, I will end it as well. It's up to you."

The Creating Power gave these people his sacred pipe. He named this land the Turtle Continent.

Then the Creating Power rested. And he wondered if he would ever have to make a fourth world.

1. *How did the Creating Power end the world the first time?*

2. *Why did the Creating Power flood the second world?*

3. *What did the Creating Power use to make the people of the third world?*

Pronunciation Guide

Every effort has been made to present native pronunciations of the unusual names in this book. Sometimes experts differed in their opinions, however, or no pronunciation could be found. Also, certain foreign-language sounds were felt to be unpronounceable by today's readers. In these cases, editorial license was exercised in selecting pronunciations.

Key

Capital letters are used to represent stressed syllables. For example, the word *ugly* would be written here as "UHG lee."

The letter or letters used to show pronunciation have the following sounds:

a as in *map* and *glad*
ah as in *pot* and *cart*
aw as in *fall* and *lost*
ch as in *chair* and *child*
e as in *let* and *care*
ee as in *feet* and *please*
ey as in *play* and *face*
g as in *gold* and *girl*

hy as in *huge* and *humor*
i as in *my* and *high*
ih as in *sit* and *clear*
j as in *jelly* and *gentle*
k as in *skill* and *can*
ky as in *cute*
l as in *long* and *pull*
my as in *mule*
ng as in *sing* and *long*
o as in *slow* and *go*
oo as in *cool* and *move*
ow as in *cow* and *round*
s as in *soon* and *cent*
sh as in *shoe* and *sugar*
th as in *thin* and *myth*
u as in *put* and *look*
uh as in *run* and *up*
y as in *you* and *yesterday*
z as in *zoo* and *pairs*

Guide

agouti: uh GOO tee
Anitsutsa:an iht SOOT suh
Apinaye: ah pih NAH ye
Arkoanyo: ahr ko AHN yo
Aztec:AZ tek
bacaba: BAH kuh buh
bayou:BAH yoo
Brulé Sioux: broo LEY SOO

Cherokee: CHER uh kee
Choctaw: CHAHK taw
Clatsop: KLAT sup
Cortes: kor TEZ
Creek: KREEK
Eskimo: ES kih mo
Galunlati: gal uhn LAH tee
gatayusti: gah tah YOOS tee
Ge: GE
Haida: HI duh
Huron: HYUR ahn
Igaluk: IHG uh luk
Kareya: kuh REY uh
Karok: KER ahk
Kiowa:KI o wuh
Klamath: KLAM uhth
Ku'ksu: KUK soo
lahal: luh HAHL
Maidu: MI doo
Modoc: MOD ahk
Montezuma: mahn te ZOO muh
Multnomah: muhlt NO muh
Narwal: NAHR wuhl
Ojibwa: o JIHB wey
Pehe-ipe: pe he EE pe
Pleiades: PLEE uh deez
Quetzalcoatl: ket sahl ko AH t'l

Rio Branco: REE o BRAHNG ko
Seminole: SEM ih nol
Sioux: SOO
Tezcatlipoca: tes kaht LEE po kuh
Tupari: TOO puh ree
Vab: VAB
Valedjad: VAL eh jahd
Wasco: WAHS ko
Yukon: YOO kahn
Yurok: YUR ahk